The Mindful Footballer: Unlocking Greatness through Meditation, Instinct, and Strategic Insight

Selasi Noamesi

Published by Selasi Noamesi, 2024.

The Mindful Footballer: Unlocking Greatness through Meditation, Instinct, and Strategic Insight

THE MINDFUL FOOTBALLER: UNLOCKING GREATNESS THROUGH MEDITATION, INSTINCT, AND STRATEGIC INSIGHT

First edition. August 11, 2024.

Copyright © 2024 Selasi Noamesi.

ISBN: 979-8227853660

Written by Selasi Noamesi.

Table of Contents

Introduction:

The Mindful Footballer: Unlocking Greatness through Meditation, Instinct, and Strategic Insight

Football is a sport that demands excellence in physical skill, tactical awareness, and mental toughness. However, the difference between a good player and a great one often lies in the unseen aspects of the game – the mental and emotional qualities that drive performance.

In today's fast-paced and competitive football landscape, players need to develop a unique combination of skills to stand out. This book will explore the often-overlooked dimensions of mindfulness, instinct, and strategic insight, and how they can be cultivated to enhance football performance.

Through a combination of meditation, self-awareness, and analytical techniques, footballers can unlock their full potential, gain a competitive edge, and become the best version of themselves on the pitch.

In the following pages, we will delve into the world of the mindful footballer, exploring the ways in which players can:

1. Develop a stronger, more focused mind through meditation and visualization

2. Tap into their instincts and intuition to make quicker, more effective decisions

3. Analyze opponents' strengths, weaknesses, and psychological profiles to gain a tactical advantage

4. Cultivate strategic insight to read the game, anticipate opponents' moves, and make informed decisions under pressure

Embracing these principles by footballers can transform their game, overcome obstacles, and achieve greatness. Let us begin the journey to unlock the mindful footballer within.

Chapter 1

Football Love Affair

The footballer must fall in love with the ball and the game. This love affair is the foundation of a lifelong journey to mastery. When a player falls in love with the ball, they:

1. Develop an unrelenting passion for the game.

2. Spend hours honing their skills, perfecting their technique.

3. Cultivate a deep understanding of the game's intricacies.

4. Build a strong bond with the ball, anticipating its every move.

5. Experience the thrill of creating something beautiful on the pitch.

6. Find joy in the journey, not just the destination.

7. Embrace the challenges, setbacks, and failures as opportunities for growth.

8. Stay committed, dedicated, and focused on their goals.

9. Inspire others with their passion, creativity, and love for the game.

10. Leave a lasting legacy, forever changing the beautiful game."

This love affair with the ball and the game is the driving force behind a footballer's success. It fuels their passion, creativity, and dedication, allowing them to reach new heights and achieve greatness.

Here are some examples of great players who fell in love with the game:

1. Lionel Messi - Known for his mesmerizing dribbling skills and goal-scoring ability, Messi's love for the game is evident in his creative playmaking and passion on the pitch.

2. Cristiano Ronaldo - A five-time Ballon d'Or winner, Ronaldo's dedication and love for the game have driven him to become one of the greatest players of all time.

3. Diego Maradona - A legendary Argentine midfielder, Maradona's love for the game was marked by his exceptional skill, vision, and leadership on the pitch.

4. Johan Cruyff - A Dutch football legend, Cruyff's love for the game was reflected in his innovative style of play, which emphasized creativity and technical skill.

5. Pelé - A three-time World Cup winner with Brazil, Pelé's love for the game was evident in his speed, skill, and scoring ability, earning him the nickname "O Rei" (The King).

6. Andres Iniesta - A Spanish midfielder, Iniesta's love for the game was marked by his exceptional vision, passing ability, and clutch performances in big games.

7. Zinedine Zidane - A French midfielder, Zidane's love for the game was reflected in his exceptional skill, vision, and leadership on the pitch, earning him the 1998 Ballon d'Or.

8. Ronaldinho - A Brazilian forward, Ronaldinho's love for the game was evident in his creative playmaking, skill, and scoring ability, earning him the 2004 and 2005 Ballon d'Or.

These players, among many others, have demonstrated a deep love and passion for the game, driving them to achieve greatness and leave a lasting impact on the beautiful game.

The Concept of Mindfulness in Football

In the context of football, mindfulness refers to the practice of being fully present, engaged, and aware of the current moment, while cultivating a non-judgmental attitude towards one's experiences on the pitch. This means that players focus their attention on the present moment, without distraction or multitasking, and observe their thoughts, feelings, and bodily sensations with curiosity and openness.

Mindfulness in football involves being aware of one's surroundings, including teammates, opponents, and the ball, while maintaining a calm and composed mindset. It requires players to accept their experiences, including mistakes and setbacks, without judgment or resistance, and to focus on the present moment, rather than dwelling on past errors or worrying about future outcomes.

By adopting a mindful approach, footballers can improve their performance, enhance their overall well-being, and gain a competitive edge. Mindfulness helps players to stay focused, composed, and adaptable under pressure, leading to better decision-making, faster reaction times, and more effective teamwork.

In the following chapters, we will explore the practical applications of mindfulness in football, including meditation, breathing exercises, and mindful movement. We will also examine the benefits of mindfulness for footballers, such as reduced stress and anxiety, improved emotional regulation, and increased self-awareness.

Integrating mindfulness into their training and match-day routines, can unlock their full potential, overcome obstacles, and achieve success in the beautiful game.

The Power of Mindfulness in Football

Mindfulness, the practice of being fully present and engaged in the current moment, has become a buzzword in modern sports. And for good reason. In football, where split-second decisions can make all the difference, mindfulness can be a game-changer. By cultivating mindfulness, players can improve their focus, situational awareness, and emotional regulation, leading to enhanced performance and a competitive edge.

The benefits of mindfulness for footballers are numerous. For one, mindfulness improves focus and concentration. By training the mind to stay present and focused, players can stay locked in on the game, even in high-pressure situations. This leads to better decision-making, faster reaction times, and a reduced likelihood of mental lapses. Additionally, mindfulness enhances situational awareness, allowing players to read the game more effectively and make more informed decisions.

Mindfulness also reduces stress and anxiety, common pitfalls for footballers. By learning to manage their emotions and stay calm under pressure, players can perform at a higher level, even in the most intense moments. Furthermore, mindfulness increases self-awareness, enabling players to better understand their strengths, weaknesses, and tendencies. This self-awareness is critical for continuous improvement and development.

So, how can footballers cultivate mindfulness? Meditation and breathing exercises are excellent starting points. Regular meditation practice trains the mind to stay present and focused, while breathing exercises calm the nervous system and reduce stress. Practical tips for integrating mindfulness into training and match-day routines include taking a few deep breaths before each play, staying focused on the present moment, and avoiding distractions.

Examples of mindful footballers abound. Players like Lionel Messi and Cristiano Ronaldo, known for their calm and focused demeanor on the pitch, are often cited as examples of mindful footballers. Their ability to stay present and focused, even in high-pressure situations, has contributed to their success.

In conclusion, mindfulness is a powerful tool for footballers. By cultivating mindfulness, players can improve their focus, situational awareness, and emotional regulation, leading to enhanced performance and a competitive edge. As the sport continues to evolve, mindfulness will become increasingly important for players seeking to gain an edge.

Chapter 2

Meditation in the Context of Football

Meditation, in the context of football, refers to a practice of training the mind to achieve a state of concentration, clarity, and inner calm. This practice involves setting aside time to focus one's attention inward, quieting the mind, and cultivating awareness of the present moment.

Through meditation, footballers can improve their concentration and focus, leading to enhanced performance on the pitch. By training the mind to stay present and aware, players can better respond to the demands of the game, making quicker decisions and reacting faster to changing situations.

Meditation also enhances emotional regulation, allowing footballers to manage stress, anxiety, and pressure more effectively. By cultivating a non-judgmental attitude towards experiences, players can develop a greater sense of self-awareness, recognizing and managing their emotions to maintain a composed mindset.

Furthermore, meditation improves mental clarity and decision-making, enabling footballers to stay focused and composed under pressure. By quieting the mind and reducing mental chatter, players can access their intuition and instincts more easily, making more informed decisions during the game.

Incorporating meditation into their training routine can provide footballers with a competitive edge, enhancing their mental toughness and resilience. Meditation is not a replacement for physical training but rather a complementary practice that can improve overall performance and contribute to success in the beautiful game.

Cultivating Focus and Concentration through Meditation

In the fast-paced and high-pressure world of football, maintaining focus and concentration is crucial for success. Meditation offers a powerful tool for footballers to cultivate these mental skills, leading to improved performance and a competitive edge.

Regular meditation practice trains the mind to stay present, focused, and aware, even in the midst of chaos. By dedicating time to meditation, footballers can develop the ability to concentrate on the task at hand, block out distractions, and maintain a calm and composed mindset under pressure.

One effective meditation technique for footballers is mindfulness meditation. This involves focusing attention on the present moment, without judgment or distraction. By paying attention to their breath, body sensations, or surroundings, footballers can cultivate a greater sense of awareness and presence.

Another technique is loving-kindness meditation, which involves cultivating compassion, empathy, and kindness towards oneself and others. This can help footballers develop a more positive mindset, build stronger relationships with teammates, and maintain a sense of calm and focus in the face of adversity.

To incorporate meditation into their training routine, footballers can start with short sessions, even just 5-10 minutes a day. Consistency is key, so it's essential to make meditation a regular habit. With regular practice, footballers can develop the mental skills necessary to perform at their best, even in the most high-pressure situations.

Through cultivation of focus and concentration through meditation, footballers can gain a mental edge, improve their performance, and unlock their full potential. In the next chapter, we will explore the power of visualization techniques in enhancing football performance.

Chapter 3

Using Visualization Techniques to Enhance Performance

Visualization is a powerful tool that can enhance football performance by harnessing the mind's ability to create vivid mental images. By vividly imagining themselves performing skills, making plays, and achieving success on the pitch, footballers can improve their confidence, focus, and overall performance.

Effective visualization involves using all the senses to create a mental picture of success. Footballers should imagine themselves executing precise passes, making sharp cuts, and scoring goals, while also incorporating sensory details like the feel of the ball, the sound of the crowd, and the smell of the grass.

Regular visualization practice can lead to improved muscle memory, enhanced spatial awareness, and increased mental toughness. By mentally rehearsing different scenarios and outcomes, footballers can prepare themselves for the demands of the game, developing a greater sense of calm and composure under pressure.

Visualization can also be used to overcome fears, doubts, and anxieties that may hold footballers back. By imagining themselves succeeding in challenging situations, players can build confidence and develop a more positive mindset, allowing them to perform at their best even in high-pressure situations.

To incorporate visualization into their training routine, footballers can set aside time each day to vividly imagine themselves performing at their best. This can be done through guided visualization exercises, self-directed mental rehearsal, or even watching videos of past successes. By leveraging the power of visualization, footballers can unlock their full potential and achieve greatness on the pitch.

Soaking Videos

Watching and studying videos of top players in their position can be incredibly beneficial for footballers. Here's why:

1. Technique: Observe and learn from the techniques used by top players, such as dribbling, passing, shooting, and ball control.

2. Decision-making: Analyze the decisions made by top players during games, including when to pass, shoot, or dribble.

3. Movement: Study the movement and positioning of top players, including their runs off the ball and spatial awareness.

4. Tactics: Understand the tactics and strategies employed by top players and their teams.

5. Inspiration: Get inspired by the skills and achievements of top players, and use that motivation to drive your own training and improvement.

6. Pattern recognition: Identify patterns and habits used by top players, and incorporate them into your own game.

7. Learning from mistakes: Even top players make mistakes - observe how they recover and learn from them.

To get the most out of watching videos:

1. Take notes and annotate the videos.

2. Slow down or pause the video to analyze specific moments.

3. Watch videos repeatedly to reinforce learning.

4. Focus on specific aspects of the game, such as technique or decision-making.

5. Compare and contrast different players and styles.

6. Apply what you've learned to your own training and games.

Chapter 4

The Concepts of Instinct and Intuition: Understanding their Role in Human Decision-Making and Behavior

Instinct and intuition are two fundamental concepts that play a crucial role in shaping human behavior and decision-making. While often used interchangeably, these terms have distinct meanings and implications. In this essay, we will delve into the definitions, characteristics, and differences between instinct and intuition, exploring their significance in various aspects of human life, including football.

Instinct refers to a natural, automatic, and unlearned response to a specific stimulus or situation. It is an innate tendency or disposition that is present from birth and is not acquired through experience or learning. Instincts are universal, automatic, and specific, triggering responses without conscious thought or deliberation. Examples of instincts include the fight or flight response, hunger and thirst drives, sexual attraction, and maternal instincts.

On the other hand, intuition is the ability to acquire knowledge or insight without conscious reasoning or deliberate thought. It is a gut feeling, hunch, or sense that something is true or will happen. Intuition is subjective, non-rational, holistic, and emergent, often arising suddenly without warning. Examples of intuition include gut feelings or hunches, creative insights or inspiration, emotional sensing or empathy, and pattern recognition or sensing connections.

A key difference between instinct and intuition lies in their origin and scope. Instincts are innate and universal, while intuition is personal and subjective. Instincts are triggered by specific stimuli, whereas intuition is often more general and holistic. Additionally, instincts are automatic, whereas intuition can be developed and refined through experience and practice.

In the context of football, instinct and intuition are essential for making quick decisions, reacting to changing situations, and performing at a high level. Players who trust their instincts and intuition can anticipate opponents' moves, sense scoring opportunities, and make informed decisions under pressure. By understanding and harnessing the power of instinct and intuition, individuals can tap into their full potential, achieving greater success and excellence in their endeavors.

Understanding Instinct and Intuition in Football

Instinct and intuition are essential components of football, enabling players to make quick decisions, react to changing situations, and perform at their best. Instinct refers to the automatic, unconscious responses that occur without deliberate thought, while intuition is the ability to acquire knowledge or insight without conscious reasoning.

In football, instinct and intuition are developed through experience, practice, and immersion in the game. Players who have spent countless hours on the pitch, honing their skills and studying the game, develop a heightened sense of awareness and instinctive understanding of the game's rhythms and patterns.

Effective footballers trust their instincts, allowing them to react quickly and decisively to emerging situations. They also cultivate their intuition, using their subconscious mind to guide their decisions and actions. By tapping into their intuition, players can anticipate opponents' moves, sense scoring opportunities, and make informed decisions under pressure.

However, instinct and intuition can be developed and refined through training and practice. Coaches and players can use drills and exercises to enhance instinctive decision-making, such as small-sided games, reaction training, and scenario-based exercises.

Moreover, players can cultivate their intuition by studying the game, analyzing opponents, and developing a deeper understanding of the game's strategic and tactical aspects. By combining instinct and intuition with deliberate practice and analysis, footballers can unlock their full potential and perform at the highest level.

The Natural World: A Source of Inspiration for Footballers

The natural world is home to a diverse range of creatures that have evolved remarkable instincts and intuition, enabling them to thrive in their environments. Footballers can learn valuable lessons from these creatures, improving their performance and decision-making on the pitch.

One of the most striking examples is the predator-prey dynamic. Lions, cheetahs, and wolves have honed their instincts to hunt and survive, exhibiting lightning-quick reflexes, adaptability, and strategic thinking. Footballers can draw parallels with these predators, developing their own instinctive abilities to anticipate opponents' movements, adapt to changing game situations, and make swift decisions during matches.

Birds of prey, such as eagles, hawks, and falcons, offer another fascinating case study. Their exceptional spatial awareness, ability to read wind patterns, and swift decision-making during hunting can inform footballers' own spatial awareness, tactical thinking, and reaction times.

Insects like ants, bees, and termites demonstrate collective intelligence, communication through chemical signals, and adaptive problem-solving. Footballers can learn from these creatures' ability to work together towards a common goal, communicate effectively, and adapt to changing circumstances.

Fish like sharks, salmon, and dolphins navigate complex environments, sensing water currents and temperature, and exhibit social learning and cooperation. Footballers can benefit from their ability to read the game's flow, adjust to changing circumstances, and work together as a cohesive unit.

Finally, migratory animals like monarch butterflies, wildebeests, and sea turtles demonstrate innate navigation systems, adaptability, and resilience. Footballers can draw inspiration from these creatures' ability to navigate challenging environments, persevere through adversity, and maintain focus on their goals.

Studying the instincts and intuition of these creatures, can help footballers gain valuable insights to enhance their performance, decision-making, and teamwork. Embracing the natural world's wisdom can help footballers unlock their full potential and achieve success on the pitch.

Chapter 5

Training Exercises to Enhance Instinctive Decision-Making

Instinctive decision-making is a crucial aspect of football, enabling players to react quickly and effectively to changing situations. While instinct is innate, it can be honed and refined through training exercises that challenge players to think and act instinctively.

One effective exercise is the "Small-Sided Game," where players participate in condensed versions of the game (e.g., 3v3 or 4v4) with reduced space and time. This forces players to make rapid decisions, relying on instinct and intuition to navigate the game's complexities.

Another exercise is "Scenario Training," where coaches simulate specific game situations, requiring players to respond instinctively. This could include scenarios like defending a counter-attack or responding to a sudden change in opponent formation.

"Reaction Training" is another valuable exercise, where players are presented with visual cues (e.g., colors, shapes) that trigger specific movements or actions. This enhances their ability to react quickly and instinctively to visual stimuli.

"Mindfulness Drills" can also be incorporated to improve instinctive decision-making. Players practice mindfulness techniques, such as focusing on their breath or body sensations, while performing football-related tasks. This trains their minds to stay present and focused, even in high-pressure situations.

Finally, "Game Situations" exercises involve presenting players with real-game scenarios, asking them to describe how they would react and make decisions. This encourages players to think critically and instinctively about the game.

Incorporating these exercises into their training routine, can enhance their instinctive decision-making, developing a more intuitive and effective playing style.

Chapter 6

Trusting Your Instincts on the Pitch

As footballers develop their instinctive abilities through training exercises, it's essential to trust their instincts during games. Trusting instincts means having faith in one's ability to make quick, effective decisions without overthinking or second-guessing.

Trusting instincts allows footballers to:

I. React faster to changing situations

II. Make more confident decisions

III. Stay focused on the present moment

IV. Avoid analysis paralysis

V. Play with more freedom and creativity

However, trusting instincts can be challenging, especially for young or inexperienced players. Fear of making mistakes, pressure from coaches or teammates, and self-doubt can hinder trust in one's instincts.

To overcome these challenges, footballers should:

I. Practice mindfulness and self-awareness to recognize and manage doubts

II. Develop a growth mindset, embracing mistakes as opportunities for growth

III. Focus on the process, not outcome, to reduce pressure and anxiety

IV. Cultivate a supportive team environment, encouraging trust and confidence

By trusting their instincts, footballers can unlock their full potential, playing with greater freedom, creativity, and effectiveness.

Atomic Practices

The footballer can achieve perfection through consistent, atomic practices. Every practice session, no matter how small, compounds upon the previous one, leading to exponential growth and mastery.

Atomic practices refer to focused, high-intensity training sessions that target specific skills or techniques. By dedicating time to these atomic practices, footballers can:

1. Build muscle memory through repetition.

2. Develop precision and accuracy.

3. Enhance their technique and skill.

4. Increase their speed and agility.

5. Improve their decision-making and reaction time.

Consistency is key. Regular atomic practices, even if just 15-20 minutes a day, can lead to significant improvements over time.

As each practice compounds upon the previous one, footballers can:

1. Develop a strong foundation in the fundamentals.

2. Progress to more complex skills and techniques.

3. Refine their game sense and instincts.

4. Achieve a high level of performance and consistency.

5. Reach perfection through persistent effort and dedication.

Examples of atomic practices include:

1. Dribbling drills with both feet

2. Shooting practice with varying levels of power and accuracy

3. Passing exercises with different types of passes (short, long, driven, etc.)

4. Agility training with cone drills or ladder exercises

5. Plyometric exercises for explosive power

By incorporating atomic practices into their daily routine, footballers can accelerate their progress, achieve perfection, and become the best version of themselves on the pitch.

Here are some examples of great players who achieved perfection through atomic practices:

1. Lionel Messi - Known for his exceptional dribbling skills, Messi spent hours as a child practicing ball control and tricks in his backyard.

2. Cristiano Ronaldo - Ronaldo's intense training sessions, including cardio, strength, and skill work, are legendary. He's a prime example of atomic practices leading to perfection.

3. Andres Iniesta - Iniesta's vision and passing ability were honed through countless hours of focused training, including drills with smaller balls and specific passing exercises.

4. Ronaldinho - Ronaldinho's creativity and skill on the ball were developed through atomic practices, including juggling, dribbling, and shooting drills.

5. Zinedine Zidane - Zidane's exceptional technique and skill were refined through focused training sessions, including specific drills for ball control, passing, and shooting.

6. Johan Cruyff - Cruyff's innovative style of play was developed through atomic practices, including exercises for ball control, vision, and passing.

7. Pele - Pele's speed, skill, and scoring ability were honed through intense training sessions, including sprints, agility drills, and shooting practice.

8. Diego Maradona - Maradona's exceptional dribbling skills and vision were developed through atomic practices, including drills with smaller balls and specific exercises for ball control.

These players, among many others, demonstrate the power of atomic practices in achieving perfection and becoming the best version of themselves on the pitch.

Chapter 7

Understanding Opponent Psychology and Behavior

Studying human psychology can help a footballer understand their opponents' behavior, decision-making, and motivations. Here are some key aspects of human psychology that can benefit a footballer:

I. Cognitive Biases: Understanding how opponents perceive and process information, including biases like confirmation bias, anchoring bias, and availability heuristic.

II. Emotional Intelligence: Recognizing and managing emotions in oneself and others, including empathy, self-awareness, and emotional regulation.

III. Motivation: Understanding what drives opponents, including intrinsic and extrinsic motivators, and how to exploit or neutralize them.

IV. Decision-Making: Knowing how opponents make decisions under pressure, including heuristics, framing effects, and risk assessment.

V. Social Influence: Understanding how opponents are influenced by their team, coach, and environment, including social norms, conformity, and persuasion.

VI. Personality Traits: Identifying individual differences in opponents, such as extraversion, agreeableness, conscientiousness, neuroticism, and openness.

VII. Learning and Memory: Understanding how opponents learn, remember, and apply tactics, including conditioning, reinforcement, and retrieval.

By studying human psychology, a footballer can:

I. Anticipate opponents' actions and decisions

II. Develop effective tactics and strategies

III. Improve communication and teamwork

IV. Enhance mental toughness and resilience

V. Gain a competitive edge through psychological insight

Remember, understanding human psychology is not about manipulating or exploiting opponents but about making informed decisions and gaining a strategic advantage.

Understanding opponent psychology and behavior is crucial in football, as it allows players and coaches to anticipate and prepare for their opponents' actions. By analyzing an opponent's mindset, tendencies, and patterns, teams can gain a competitive edge and make informed decisions during the game.

Once again, opponent's psychology encompasses various factors, including:

I. Motivation: Understanding what drives an opponent, such as their strengths, weaknesses, and goals.

II. Emotional State: Recognizing an opponent's emotional state, like confidence, anxiety, or aggression.

III. Tactical Approach: Identifying an opponent's playing style, formations, and strategies.

IV. Player Personalities: Understanding individual player traits, like leadership, work rate, or technical ability.

V. Team Dynamics: Analyzing the relationships and communication within the opposing team.

By emphasis, by studying these factors, teams can develop effective game plans, exploit opponent weaknesses, and neutralize their strengths. This knowledge also enables players to make better decisions during the game, such as:

I. Anticipating opponent movements and actions

II. Identifying opportunities to press or drop back

III. Selecting the right moments to take risks or play safe

IV. Adapting to changing opponent tactics or emotions

V. Executing set pieces and counter-attacks more effectively

In conclusion, understanding opponent psychology and behavior is essential for success in football. By gathering and analyzing this information, teams can gain a deeper understanding of their opponents and make informed decisions to outmaneuver them.

Chapter 8

Analyzing Physiological Strengths and Weaknesses

In addition to understanding opponent psychology, analyzing physiological strengths and weaknesses is crucial in football. This involves examining the physical attributes and capabilities of individual opponents, including:

I. Speed and Agility: Quickness, acceleration, and change of direction

II. Endurance and Stamina: Aerobic capacity, anaerobic threshold, and recovery rate

III. Strength and Power: Muscular force, explosiveness, and resistance to fatigue

IV. Flexibility and Mobility: Range of motion, flexibility, and movement fluidity

V. Injury Proneness: History of injuries, vulnerability to specific injuries, and current fitness level

By analyzing these physiological factors, footballers can:

I. Identify opponents' strengths and weaknesses

II. Develop targeted tactics to exploit weaknesses

III. Prepare effective counter-measures to neutralize opponents' strengths

IV. Enhance their own physiological capabilities through training

V. Make informed decisions about player selection, positioning, and substitution

Physiological analysis also helps footballers understand how opponents adapt to different situations, such as:

I. Fatigue and recovery patterns

II. Response to high-intensity efforts

III. Adaptation to changing environmental conditions

IV. Effects of travel, altitude, and climate on performance

Understanding Physiological Limitations to Neutralize Opponents

A footballer must also understand the capabilities and limitations of the human body to develop skills that can neutralize their opponents' physical abilities. This includes recognizing the boundaries of:

I. Reflexes: Reaction time, speed, and accuracy

II. Speed and Agility: Acceleration, deceleration, and change of direction

III. Endurance and Stamina: Aerobic capacity, anaerobic threshold, and recovery rate

IV. Strength and Power: Muscular force, explosiveness, and resistance to fatigue

V. Flexibility and Mobility: Range of motion, flexibility, and movement fluidity

By understanding these physiological limitations, footballers can develop strategies to:

I. Exploit opponents' slow reaction times or limited agility

II. Utilize speed and endurance to outmaneuver opponents

III. Employ strength and power to overpower opponents

IV. Leverage flexibility and mobility to evade opponents' tackles

V. Anticipate and prepare for opponents' physical responses

For example, a footballer can develop skills to neutralize an opponent's quick reflexes by:

I. Using feints and decoy movements to create uncertainty

II. Employing speed and agility to create separation

III. Utilizing strength and power to shield the ball

IV. Exploiting opponents' momentary lapses in concentration

V. Anticipating and reacting to opponents' predictable responses

When footballers combine physiological analysis with psychological insights, they can gain a comprehensive understanding of their opponents, making them better equipped to succeed on the pitch.

Pushing Physiological Boundaries through Training

While understanding physiological limitations is crucial, footballers should also strive to push their bodies beyond natural boundaries through dedicated training. This involves:

I. Neurological Training: Enhancing reaction time, speed, and accuracy through cognitive exercises and drills

II. Conditioning and Endurance: Expanding aerobic capacity, anaerobic threshold, and recovery rate through targeted cardio and strength training

III. Strength and Power Development: Building muscular force, explosiveness, and resistance to fatigue through resistance training and plyometrics

IV. Flexibility and Mobility Enhancement: Increasing range of motion, flexibility, and movement fluidity through stretching, mobility exercises, and functional training

V. Injury Prevention and Management: Strengthening vulnerable areas, improving flexibility, and developing strategies for rapid recovery

By pushing their bodies beyond natural boundaries, footballers can:

I. Achieve faster reaction times and quicker decision-making

II. Maintain high-intensity efforts over longer periods

III. Deliver more powerful shots, passes, and tackles

IV. Evade opponents with greater ease and agility

V. Recover faster from injuries and fatigue

For example, a footballer can train to:

I. Improve reaction time through cognitive training and drills

II. Increase speed and endurance through sprint interval training and cardio exercises

III. Enhance strength and power through resistance band training and plyometrics

IV. Develop flexibility and mobility through dynamic stretching and functional training

V. Strengthen vulnerable areas through targeted injury prevention exercises

Through pushing their physiological boundaries, footballers can gain a competitive edge, achieve exceptional performance, and redefine what is thought possible.

Chapter 9

Mastering the Art of Adaptation and Evolution

In the dynamic and unpredictable world of football, adaptation and evolution are crucial for success. Footballers must be able to adjust their strategies, tactics, and techniques to stay ahead of their opponents and respond to changing circumstances.

I. Embracing Flexibility: Being open to new ideas, strategies, and tactics

II. Analyzing Opponent Adaptations: Recognizing and responding to opponents' adjustments

III. Evolving Tactics: Introducing new formations, strategies, and plays to stay ahead

IV. Developing Versatility: Acquiring new skills and abilities to expand playing options

V. Staying Ahead of the Curve: Anticipating and preparing for future developments and innovations

By mastering the art of adaptation and evolution, footballers can:

I. Stay competitive in a rapidly changing environment

II. Outmaneuver opponents through innovative tactics and strategies

III. Enhance their skills and abilities through continuous learning

IV. Build resilience and confidence through adaptability

V. Achieve long-term success and dominance in the sport

For example, a footballer can:

I. Adjust their playing style to suit different opponents and situations

II. Develop new skills and techniques to expand their playing options

III. Introduce novel tactics and strategies to catch opponents off guard

IV. Analyze opponents' adaptations and adjust their approach accordingly

V. Stay up-to-date with the latest developments and innovations in the sport

Through adaptation and evolution, footballers can thrive in the dynamic and competitive world of football.

Chapter 10

The Power of Mental Resilience in Football

Mental resilience is a critical component of success in football. It enables players to perform at their best, even in the face of adversity, pressure, and failure. By developing mental resilience, footballers can:

I. Overcome Fear and Doubt: Build confidence and self-belief to perform at their best

II. Manage Pressure and Stress: Develop coping strategies to handle the demands of the game

III. Bounce Back from Setbacks: Learn from mistakes and failures, and use them as opportunities for growth

IV. Stay Focused and Motivated: Maintain concentration and drive, even in the face of adversity

V. Build Strong Team Dynamics: Foster a positive and supportive team culture

By cultivating mental resilience, footballers can:

I. Enhance their performance and achieve their goals

II. Develop a growth mindset and continuously improve

III. Build strong relationships with teammates and coaches

IV. Navigate the challenges of the game with confidence and poise

V. Achieve long-term success and fulfillment in their careers

For example, a footballer can:

I. Use visualization techniques to build confidence and prepare for games

II. Practice mindfulness and meditation to manage pressure and stress

III. Develop a growth mindset by learning from mistakes and failures

IV. Set goals and work towards them with focus and determination

V. Build strong relationships with teammates through open communication and support

Through the idea of prioritizing mental resilience, footballers can unlock their full potential and achieve success in the beautiful game.

Chapter 11

The Importance of Continuous Learning and Improvement

In the ever-evolving sport of football, continuous learning and improvement are essential for success. Footballers must stay up-to-date with the latest developments, trends, and innovations to remain competitive. By embracing a culture of continuous learning, footballers can:

I. Stay Ahead of the Curve: Anticipate and adapt to changes in the game

II. Enhance Their Skills: Develop new techniques, tactics, and strategies

III. Improve Their Decision-Making: Analyze situations, learn from mistakes, and make informed decisions

IV. Expand Their Knowledge: Study the game, opponents, and themselves to gain a deeper understanding

V. Foster a Growth Mindset: Embrace challenges, learn from failures, and continuously improve

By prioritizing continuous learning and improvement, footballers can:

I. Achieve Long-Term Success: Stay relevant and competitive throughout their careers

II. Develop a Competitive Edge: Stay ahead of opponents and adapt to changing circumstances

III. Enhance Their Enjoyment: Continuously challenge themselves and find joy in the learning process

IV. Build Resilience: Develop coping strategies and learn from setbacks

V. Inspire Others: Set an example for teammates, coaches, and future generations

For example, a footballer can:

I. Attend workshops, clinics, and conferences to learn from experts

II. Analyze game footage, statistics, and data to improve their performance

III. Seek feedback from coaches, teammates, and mentors

IV. Read books, articles, and research papers to expand their knowledge

V. Experiment with new techniques, tactics, and strategies in training sessions

As footballers engage continuous learning and improvement, they can unlock their full potential, achieve success, and leave a lasting legacy in the beautiful game.

Chapter 12

The Role of Technology in Football Development

Technology has revolutionized the sport of football, transforming the way players train, teams prepare, and coaches strategize. By embracing technology, footballers can:

I. Enhance Performance Analysis: Utilize data analytics and video analysis to improve technique and tactics

II. Optimize Training Methods: Leverage technology-based training tools and equipment for more effective practice

III. Improve Injury Prevention: Use advanced medical technology and data analysis to predict and prevent injuries

IV. Develop Virtual Training Environments: Utilize virtual and augmented reality to simulate game situations and enhance decision-making

V. Facilitate Communication and Collaboration: Employ digital platforms to connect with teammates, coaches, and mentors

By integrating technology into their development, footballers can:

I. Gain a Competitive Edge: Stay ahead of opponents through data-driven insights and technology-enhanced training

II. Improve Efficiency: Streamline training and preparation through technology-based tools and methods

III. Enhance Player Safety: Reduce injury risk through advanced medical technology and data analysis

IV. Expand Access to Resources: Connect with global experts, coaches, and mentors through digital platforms

V. Future-Proof Their Careers: Develop skills and adaptability for an ever-changing football landscape

For example, a footballer can:

I. Use wearable technology to track performance metrics and optimize training

II. Analyze game footage using AI-powered video analysis software

III. Engage in virtual reality training sessions to simulate game scenarios

IV. Collaborate with coaches and teammates through digital communication platforms

V. Utilize data analytics to identify areas for improvement and track progress

Footballers, through technology, can revolutionize their development, gain a competitive edge, and succeed in the modern game.

Chapter 13

The Importance of Nutrition and Recovery in Football

Proper nutrition and recovery are crucial components of a footballer's success. A well-planned diet and effective recovery strategies can:

I. Enhance Performance: Fuel the body for optimal energy, speed, and endurance

II. Support Injury Prevention: Strengthen muscles, bones, and connective tissues to reduce injury risk

III. Aid in Injury Recovery: Accelerate the healing process through targeted nutrition and recovery techniques

IV. Improve Mental Clarity: Fuel the brain for focus, concentration, and decision-making

V. Support Long-Term Health: Foster healthy habits for a lifetime of wellness

By prioritizing nutrition and recovery, footballers can:

I. Gain a Competitive Edge: Outperform opponents through optimized energy and performance

II. Reduce Injury Risk: Strengthen their body and reduce downtime due to injury

III. Speed Up Recovery: Get back to training and competition faster after injuries or intense matches

IV. Improve Mental Toughness: Develop resilience and focus through proper nutrition and recovery

V. Extend Their Career: Support long-term health and performance through sustainable habits

For example, a footballer can:

I. Consult a sports dietitian to create a personalized nutrition plan

II. Incorporate recovery techniques like foam rolling, stretching, and self-myofascial release

III. Prioritize sleep and aim for 7-9 hours of restful sleep each night

IV. Use nutrition and recovery tracking tools to monitor progress and adjust strategies

V. Make healthy lifestyle choices, such as staying hydrated and managing stress

When nutrition and recovery, is emphasized for

footballers, they can unlock their full potential, achieve success, and maintain long-term health and wellness.

Chapter 14

Integrating Mindfulness, Instinct, and Strategic Insight into Your Game

The beautiful game of football requires a harmonious blend of mindfulness, instinct, and strategic insight. By integrating these three elements, footballers can unlock their full potential and achieve success on the pitch.

I. Mindfulness: The Foundation

Mindfulness is the foundation of this synergy. It enables players to stay present, focused, and aware of their surroundings. Through mindfulness practices such as meditation and deep breathing, footballers can:

II. Enhance Situational Awareness

III. Improve Decision-Making

IV. Reduce Stress and Anxiety

V. Instinct: Trusting Your Inner Voice

Instinct is the natural ability to react swiftly and effectively in high-pressure situations. It is developed through experience, intuition, and trust in one's abilities. By trusting their instincts, footballers can:

VI. Make Split-Second Decisions with Confidence

VII. Anticipate Opponents' Moves

VIII. Execute Skills with Precision and Flair

IX. Strategic Insight: Reading the Game

Strategic insight is the ability to read the game, anticipate patterns, and make informed decisions. It is developed through analysis, experience, and knowledge of the game. By combining strategic insight with mindfulness and instinct, footballers can:

X. Execute Tactics with Purpose and Intention

XI. Adapt to Changing Circumstances

XII. Outmaneuver Opponents

By integrating mindfulness, instinct, and strategic insight, footballers can:

XIII. Make Informed Decisions with Clarity and Precision

XIV. Trust Their Instincts to React Swiftly and Effectively

XV. Execute Strategies with Purpose and Intention

By cultivating this synergy, footballers can:

XVI. Enhance Their Overall Performance

XVII. Gain a Competitive Edge

XVIII. Achieve Success and Fulfillment in Their Careers

Chapter 15

Overcoming Mental and Physical Challenges

Footballers face numerous mental and physical challenges that can impact their performance and well-being. These challenges can include:

I. Pressure to Perform

II. Fear of Failure

III. Physical Injuries

IV. Mental Fatigue

V. Self-Doubt

To overcome these obstacles, footballers can:

VI. Develop Coping Strategies

VII. Leverage Support Networks

VIII. Focus on Progress, Not Perfection

By adopting this approach, footballers can:

IX. Build Mental Toughness

X. Foster Emotional Intelligence

XI. Maintain Physical and Mental Health

XII. Develop Resilience Techniques

XIII. Learn from Failures

XIV. Stay Motivated

XV. Cultivate a Positive Mindset

By overcoming mental and physical challenges, footballers can:

XVI. Enhance Their Performance

XVII. Achieve Success and Fulfillment

XVIII. Maintain a Long-Term Career

XIX. Build Strong Relationships

XX. Stay Adaptable and Responsive

By integrating these strategies, footballers can overcome mental and physical challenges and reach their full potential.

Chapter 16

Maintaining a Growth Mindset and Continuous Improvement

A growth mindset is the foundation for continuous improvement and success in football. By embracing this mindset, players can:

I. Embrace Challenges

II. View Failures as Opportunities

III. Cultivate a Love for Learning

IV. Stay Curious and Open to New Experiences

V. Focus on Progress, Not Perfection

By maintaining a growth mindset, footballers can:

VI. Stay Adaptable and Responsive

VII. Continuously Refine Their Skills and Knowledge

VIII. Achieve Long-Term Success and Fulfillment

IX. Develop a Resilient and Growth-Oriented Mindset

X. Enhance Their Creativity and Resourcefulness

XI. Build Strong Relationships with Coaches and Teammates

XII. Stay Motivated and Focused

XIII. Overcome Mental and Physical Challenges

XIV. Reach Their Full Potential

XV. Achieve a High Level of Performance and Success

By integrating a growth mindset and continuous improvement, footballers can:

XVI. Stay Ahead of the Competition

XVII. Achieve Sustained Success

XVIII. Build a Lasting Legacy

XIX. Inspire Others with Their Passion and Dedication

XX. Continuously Evolve and Improve.

By way of emphasis, the footballer's talent can be enhanced to its heights intelligently through:

1. Deliberate Practice: Focus on specific aspects of performance, with structured and purposeful training.

2. Expert Guidance: Work with experienced coaches, mentors, or trainers who can provide personalized feedback and direction.

3. Intelligent Training: Use data, analytics, and technology to optimize training methods and track progress.

4. Holistic Development: Address physical, mental, and emotional aspects of performance to achieve well-rounded growth.

5. Continuous Learning: Stay curious, seek new knowledge, and adapt to changing circumstances.

6. Strategic Planning: Set clear goals, prioritize efforts, and make informed decisions to maximize progress.

7. Resilience and Adaptability: Develop coping skills, learn from failures, and adjust to new challenges.

8. Performance Psychology: Apply mental skills training, such as visualization, mindfulness, and self-talk, to enhance performance.

9. Nutrition and Recovery: Fuel the body with optimal nutrition and prioritize recovery techniques to support intense training.

10. Innovation and Creativity: Encourage experimentation, explore new techniques, and find innovative solutions to improve performance.

Once again, by taking a thoughtful and multi-faceted approach, individuals can intelligently enhance their talent, achieve their full potential, and reach new heights of success.

Conclusion:

The beautiful game of football is a journey of self-discovery, growth, and excellence. By integrating the following principles, footballers can unlock their full potential and achieve success:

1. Integrate mindfulness, instinct, and strategic insight to enhance performance.

2. Overcome mental and physical challenges to build resilience.

3. Maintain a growth mindset to continuously improve and adapt.

4. Cultivate a resilient and growth-oriented mindset to stay motivated.

5. Build mental toughness and emotional intelligence to perform under pressure.

6. Foster a positive and solution-focused mindset to overcome obstacles.

7. Maintain physical and mental health to ensure longevity.

8. Stay adaptable and responsive to changing circumstances.

9. Continuously refine skills and knowledge to stay ahead.

10. Achieve long-term success and fulfillment in their careers.

By embracing these principles, footballers can:

1. Enhance their situational awareness and adaptability.

2. Amplify their creativity and resourcefulness.

3. Build strong relationships with coaches and teammates.

4. Stay motivated and focused.

5. Overcome mental and physical challenges.

6. Reach their full potential.

7. Achieve a high level of performance and success.

8. Stay ahead of the competition.

9. Achieve sustained success.

10. Build a lasting legacy.

Remember, the beautiful game is not just about winning or losing, but about the journey of self-discovery, growth, and excellence.

Here are some quotes from some great players and coaches in the context of this book:

I. "The ball is my best friend." - Lionel Messi

(Emphasizing the importance of developing a deep connection with the ball through consistent practice)

II. "I never stopped believing in myself." - Cristiano Ronaldo

(Highlighting the power of self-belief and resilience in overcoming obstacles)

III. "Football is a game of mistakes. Whoever makes the fewest mistakes wins." - Johan Cruyff

(Underlining the importance of learning from mistakes and continuous improvement)

IV. "The greatest glory in living lies not in never falling, but in rising every time we fall." - Nelson Mandela (quoted by Pep Guardiola)

(Emphasizing the value of resilience and perseverance in overcoming setbacks)

V. "I don't just train my body, I train my mind." - Andres Iniesta

(Highlighting the importance of mental preparation and focus in achieving success)

VI. "The key is to be consistent, to always be at a high level." - Zinedine Zidane

(Underlining the importance of consistent effort and dedication in achieving greatness)

VII. "You can't buy experience, but you can learn from it." - Sir Alex Ferguson

(Emphasizing the value of learning from experience and continuous growth)

VIII. "The most important thing is to always be able to adapt." - Diego Maradona

(Highlighting the importance of adaptability and flexibility in responding to changing circumstances)

ABOUT THE AUTHOR

Selasi Evans Noamesi is an anointed man of God who operates in the dynamics of God's power, in healing, miracles and the prophetic. He is a dynamic teacher of the Word of God, bringing fresh insights and revelations from the heart of God in the Bible, through the lens of the Cross of Christ, to the Body of Christ. He is the founder of the Eternal Assembly of Christ, a ministry currently in Ghana, West Africa.

He is a prolific writer who has PhD in Theology.

Contact Information: call/WhatsApp +233241227470/ +233204897476

Facebook: Apostle Selasi E.N Epiphanes / Selasi Evans Noamesi